Susan Macfarlane 1938–2002

To Susan's grandchildren; that they may draw from her free spirit.

Foreword

When someone dies unexpectedly, there is a natural urge to find ways to make up for the loss; and, if that person were unusually creative, to try to amass and document that creativity in an effort to understand its origins. Susan probably produced over 700 oil paintings, and many more drawings, during her lifetime. Those that we have selected illustrate the tremendous diversity in her work, spanning a career that took root in South Asia during the 1960s, and ended, almost back where it began, with a return to India some 40 years later.

Euan and Angus Mackay

July 2005

Contents

The life of a painter

Early years

Susan Macfarlane was born in West Sussex in the summer of 1938, moving soon afterwards to her childhood home in Hampshire. She was too young to remember much about World War II, yet Hampton Hill Cottage was only a few miles away from Southampton docks and therefore not entirely out of harm's way. Blissfully unaware of the dangers, Susan, calling out 'Bangs, Mummy, bangs', would get up with great excitement during the small hours of the morning to sit out the air raids; milk and biscuits were usually on offer, too! On one occasion she had to be carried kicking and screaming indoors from her swing, only for there to be found (a few hours later) pieces of shrapnel lying about the garden – one of which had landed on the swing itself.

Susan's childhood was very social in a typically English-country sort of way. The family was close, and both children received all the support that their parents could provide. Malcolm[1], her father, could often appear stern and disciplinarian, but he and Susan had a special rapport and his letters to her in later years reveal a sensitive and caring nature. Her mother, Mary, was intelligent and vivacious with a world view that did not always sit well with her life as a farmer's wife. A graduate of agriculture (University College, Reading), she was better educated than most of her peers and held political views closely aligned with the Women's Rights movement of the time.

Susan's talent for drawing was quite developed even as a young child – it was all she ever wanted to do. She would lean against a fence or a gate for hours, apparently totally idle, but she was always observing – objects, colours, light and movement. She did 'all right' at school, but inspiration came mainly from her drawing and her love of animals. So she was only too delighted to be released from purgatory at the age of 16 and to enrol at the Winchester School of Art. This period was critical to her future development as a painter, most likely confirming in her own mind, and perhaps also in that of her teacher[2], that she had the necessary talent.

By the time Susan was 18, Mary Macfarlane had prevailed on her to get out and earn a living (something that her painting was unlikely to deliver at this stage), so she joined the War Office[3] as a shorthand typist. Those early days in Warwick Road (West London) were dominated by parties, coffee bars and concerts – painting was reserved for her spare time. The most memorable examples of her work at this stage are the caricatures of War Office colleagues. Few were spared the pen, least of all the senior civil servants and 'spymasters' for whom Susan worked.

9

---

[1] Malcolm Macfarlane MC (1889–1975) – He started his career as an apprentice for Rolls Royce before joining the Royal Engineers in 1914. During World War I he was awarded the Military Cross at Cambrai in November 1917. On his return from France he then devoted his time to farming in Sussex and Hampshire, marrying Mary in 1925. In retirement he set up his own metal and woodwork business.

[2] Susan had a lot of respect for David Pare, always mentioning his name in her résumé.
[3] The Ministry of Defence.

Ceylon, East Asia and Greece

Although Britain's Empire and influence were rapidly waning in the post-war years, it still retained certain key responsibilities around the world. For Susan it was a case of being in the right place at the right time when one of her co-workers turned down the opportunity of a posting to Ceylon[4]. She never said much about the work, but then it wasn't the job that she was interested in – rather the intensity, colour and velvet texture of the tropics. It was an astonishingly beautiful place and an enormously exciting experience for a relatively naïve 22-year-old from England. Susan lived in splendour (at least by Warwick Road standards), sharing an HM Government flat with Angela Winter[5]. Weekends were spent exploring endless beaches, at the yacht club or cooling off 'up-country'. They climbed Adam's Peak, rising 7000 ft above the tea estates, camped in the jungle and drank Champagne in the sea.

Susan held several exhibitions while in Ceylon. The first of these took place at home and included not only a series of her paintings but a frieze of Ceylon crows carefully stencilled on to one of the RSJs! At the last minute Susan announced that she would rather be elsewhere, leaving Angela to cope with the guests, including a suspicious-minded Deputy High Commissioner with an eye for inappropriate 'artistic improvements'. The second exhibition was an altogether more auspicious affair at the Times of Ceylon Gallery in the centre of Colombo, which was well attended and received coverage in the national newspapers. Susan sold much of what she had produced and, of course, there is nothing quite like a sale to boost confidence. It may have been these early successes that finally convinced her to paint full-time.

She was still very young and inevitably unsure about whether the dream could be realized, but had obviously decided to give 'chance' a shove. Although her parents were hardly conservative by nature, the decision to resign from her 'job for life' led to a certain amount of chagrin and Susan wisely decided to ride out the storm in Asia, staying with friends in Singapore and travelling on to Thailand, Malaysia, Cambodia[6] and Hong Kong. In Malaysia she spent some time in Penang, from where she wrote on a postcard home: 'It is pelting with rain. The water is a rich grey-green and the boats seem only red and black in the deluge.' No masterpiece of literacy, but quite clearly the writing of a painter.

On her way back to England at the end of 1962, Susan stopped off at the artists' island of Hydra in the southern Aegean where she met the Greek painter John Dragoumis. He was an outspoken critic who was quick to offer good advice, which Susan was equally quick to put to good use. Dragoumis, clearly delighted with his protégée, introduced her to his English friend, William Burman, a writer who had recently settled on the island. Susan decided to return the following year to paint, and William offered her the use of the annexe to his house on the condition that she would paint him a picture. There she set up her studio, using it as a base from which to explore the island day after day, sketching people, boats and scenery. This turned out to be a formative period for Susan, during which she progressed from a person with a love of drawing into an artist able to use colour, form, texture and

[4] Former name for Sri Lanka until 1972.
[5] Angela Winter (married Commander R. Angel RN) remained a close family friend.
[6] Susan visited Angkor Wat in 1962. At that time there were no tourists; she saw a few monks and met a solitary French archaeologist. There were visible bullet holes in the masonry of many of the temples.
[7] Ronald Gordon Mackay (1901–1991) – He joined the Royal Navy in 1913, seeing active service during World War II on *HMS Ark Royal* and *HMS Rodney*. He retired as a senior Captain in 1952, pursuing a second career with Foster Wheeler and Clyde Blowers until the age of 70.

[8] In fact Michael and Ronald got on very well, and the former's comment served only to highlight that even though this *was* an extraordinary decision, he was not overly surprised.
[9] During her Warwick Road years Susan had helped at the Mayflower Family Centre in Canning Town (East London) – a Christian mission run at that time by David Sheppard (the England cricketer and future Bishop of Liverpool, who died March 2005). But it was the larger-than-life figure of Sheppard's deputy, George Burton, who influenced Susan most and with whom she continued to correspond in later life.
[10] The Holy Trinity Church, 2–4 Rue General Ferrie, 06400 Cannes, France.

space in original ways. The painting which she eventually produced for William, *The Rocks*, p.41, set the tone for much that was to follow.

Cannes and Provence

Perhaps one of the more unusual facts of Susan's life is that, in 1964, she married a man 37 years older than herself. At the age of 62, Ronald Mackay[7], a widower, had both the energy to start all over again and the audacity to propose to a 25-year-old. Mary Macfarlane was distraught, as any parent with the future interests of a child might justifiably be, while brother Michael declared: 'Oh well, Susan always was a bit odd.'[8] Susan was undoubtedly attracted to Ronald's intellect and internationalism, but she too had her concerns and wrote to friend and mentor George Burton[9] about the decision that she was about to make. His response was straight to the heart of the matter: 'My advice to the both of you is that you are marrying each other, not relations or friends.' Ronald himself had no doubts at all and set about rearranging his life with gusto. Children came quickly: Euan was born in 1965 and Angus two years later.

The first major artistic project that came Susan's way was the design of stained-glass windows for Holy Trinity, the new Anglican church in Cannes[10]. It was to rock formations that she returned for inspiration, producing a series of *maquettes* for submission to the church committee – nervous moments indeed. Next came the complex and painstaking process of converting concept to reality, for which, as luck would have it, the church managed to engage possibly the best master glazier on the Riviera, Alain Peinado. With the

Susan at the age of 3¾

Out riding with the local hunt – Susan strays from the field

Susan and her brother Michael

Susan with her mother Mary at Hampton Hill Cottage

11

aid of Patrick Reyntiens's book, *The Technique of Stained Glass*, they toiled for months in Alain's crowded 'back-streets-of-Nice' workshop, finally completing the main *dalles de verre* at the west end of the church in 1973. A few years – and several hundred cups of espresso – later, they finished the project with a set of clerestory windows depicting scenes from the Old Testament. It was good work and very well executed. Susan learned a huge amount and would quite happily have continued to work in stained glass for many years to come. Sadly such commissions are rare, and she was never able to work in this medium again. She did, however, keep up her interest in glass and gave several talks on the subject later on in her life, one of which is reproduced in full on pages 125–29.

The rock studies that formed the basis of Susan's designs for Holy Trinity in Cannes were inspired by the dramatic alpine hinterland to which she and Ronald had become increasingly attached, and where they eventually built a holiday cottage near Comps-sur-Artuby in 1970[11]. This rugged landscape matured the techniques that Susan had learned on Hydra. She explored concepts of time, space and nature in its most elemental forms, through the rock formations and tree shapes. After a while there was not a hill in the area that she had not studied and documented (usually from several different angles), often featuring the many ruined farmsteads and chapels that litter this landscape. She was particularly drawn to the Chapelle de St Thyr[12] on the road between Comps and Castellane, and produced many drawings and several paintings of this site set against the imposing mass of the Montagne de Robion.

The Cotswolds

By the early 1980s both children were at boarding school in England and Ronald, though still physically and mentally fit, was of an age that demanded a degree of forward planning. He and Susan bought an old house in Wiltshire[13], using it as their base during the winter months. Susan continued to paint her beloved mountains of the Basses Alpes during the summer, but it was to the prehistoric downlands of southern Britain that she was drawn for the rest of the year. Like many artists before her, Susan was fascinated by the thousands of years of human history visible in these landscapes. She once remarked: 'Every tree that you see has either been placed there or left there by man.' The great Henge monuments of the late Stone Age and early Bronze Age were particularly captivating – none more so than Avebury. Susan painted a whole series of paintings there, transposing the vitality of modern life on to the massive and timeless Sarsen stones[14].

This influence in Susan's life was perhaps a continuation of a theme that she had already begun to explore in France with *La Pierre de la Fée et sa Maison*, p.55, a 1500 BC dolmen[15]. That portrayal, which features an unremarkable Provençal red-tile house in the background, faces the opposite way from touristy photographs, unequivocally placing the stones within the context of the modern era. The imagery advocates, more effectively than words ever could, Susan's abiding beliefs in the cyclical nature of life.

The Mackays moved to England permanently in 1986, immediately – and somewhat rashly –

---

[11] Au Vieux Pont, La Souche, Comps-sur-Artuby.
[12] The Government apparently agreed that the site was worth preserving and in the mid-1980s set about its restoration; the work was carried out with great sensitivity and skill.
[13] Stonehaven, a 16th-century wool merchant's house in Biddestone, near Chippenham.
[14] Sarsen stones are large exposed blocks of sandstone left on the surface of the landscape through glacial processes and then incorporated by Stone Age people into their monuments and burial chambers.
[15] Datant de l'époque chalcolithique de Provence (1500–1000 avant JC), ce dolmen appelé la Pierre de la Fée est situé à 1 km au Nord-Ouest de Draguignan.
[16] Red Lion House, Swells Hill, Brimscombe, Gloucestershire.

getting embroiled in renovating a decrepit and 'ill-loved' Jacobean farmhouse in the Cotswolds[16]. The house required a huge amount of work and took about three years to complete, by which time Ronald was in need of continuous care. Yet Susan managed to sustain her painting through this difficult period, working on a portrayal of people at work in the wool mills of the Stroud Valley.

During the 18th and 19th centuries this picturesque part of south Gloucestershire had been a thriving industrial zone producing high-quality cloth. A network of canals and remarkable tunnels through the chalk connected the mills with their markets in Bristol, Oxford and London. By the mid-1990s just one operating mill remained, the others long since consigned to 'character of the landscape' status, alongside the boggy remains of the waterways that had once sustained them. Even the Longford's Mill, the centrepiece of Susan's subsequent exhibition in 1992, has now closed. However, at that time cloth was still being made there, in a curious fusion of people and machines amid luminous colour: snooker-table green, Wimbledon tennis-ball yellow, and the eye-catching purples and reds of guardsmen's cloaks.

Ronald Mackay died in 1991 after a marriage that had lasted 27 years. It had not been easy towards the end, but the relationship had been a success. Susan mourned his passing with a quiet intensity hidden from all but her closest friends, for she had deeply loved and respected this unconventional man with his Edwardian upbringing yet liberal views and modernity. The inevitable had happened, as she had always known it would.

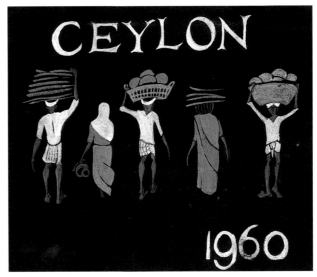

Memories of Ceylon (front cover of Susan's photo album)

New Year's Eve, Colombo 1961

Cartoon of Naval Officer, Hong Kong 1962

13

A new beginning

With change came the opportunity to produce more work and to exhibit. Instinctively Susan chose to show the mill paintings locally rather than opting for a more prestigious location. It was a gamble that, in her own mind, paid off. Her work was far removed from the 'norm' for a small country town, but local people came to the exhibition appreciating the fact that someone had recorded the human dimension of a defining piece of local history[17]. Even the District Council became involved, persuading a rather bemused Susan to travel to Germany as part of a town-twinning extravaganza between Stroud and Göttingen, Lower Saxony.

Over the next few years Susan documented, in a manner similar to that of the mills, the process of whisky-making in the north of Scotland[18], and visited the Island of Gozo to explore the neolithic temples at Gigantija. This was perhaps a partial throwback to the Wiltshire days, and resulted in a collection of remarkably vivid paintings reflecting the mysticism of imagined ancient people set against the intense heat of the Mediterranean. It was at Gigantija that Susan came across the ancient symbol for renewal of life, which she later used as a dimension to her paintings of cancer care[19].

This succession of exhibitions established Susan as a Gloucestershire artist[20]. She was much in demand, which helped greatly in adjusting

to widowhood. At about this time she met Dr Geoffrey Farrer-Brown, a histopathologist, who on hearing about the success of the mills exhibition invited Susan to produce a series of paintings on breast cancer. The aim was to help to demystify the disease by showing the pathway down which a patient travels, from the first consultation, through examinations, treatment and recovery. The concept intrigued Susan: a stark working place dealing with critical diagnostic decisions, yet filled with a hidden emotion.

Her collaboration with Farrer-Brown over the next four years resulted in an extraordinarily original and groundbreaking exhibition. It was without question the best of Susan to date, and quite without precedent either medically or artistically. It was also a huge gamble which might have attracted a lot of criticism and little else, but after a lifetime in medicine Farrer-Brown quite clearly had the courage of his convictions. 'A Picture of Health' was duly launched at the Barbican Centre in London in early 1995, and was followed by a seven-city UK tour. A decade later, the exhibition is still on tour and at time of writing has been exhibited in no fewer than 40 places – a record in itself.

There are those who remain sceptical about the value of art to the suffering of cancer patients and their families, but both then and now the overwhelming majority are supportive. Letters flooded in, countless articles appeared in the media (both local and national) and the project was featured on a BBC frontline news programme[21]. The exhibition propelled

[17] This was also a significant chapter in Britain's national industrial heritage.

[18] She returned each evening to her lodgings technically 'over the limit' from alcoholic fumes inhaled during the day at the Balblair distillery.

[19] The 'Tree of Life' is shaped like the mathematical sign for infinity, most likely drawn from ancient Western iconography and denoting the perpetual cyclical renewal of life.

[20] Susan responded by giving her time as Arts Adviser to the Gloucester NHS Trust, and to the Royal West of England Academy as Committee Member and Treasurer.

[21] *Newsnight* with Jeremy Paxman.

Susan into the public eye for a short while, her work inspiring national interest.

Farrer-Brown went on to expand his concept of art and health. He succeeded in convincing Susan to stay involved, this time recording children and their families living with leukaemia. One of the most moving paintings produced by Susan, entitled *After Alice*, p.105, depicts a father, mother and their young son watching a home video of their daughter in life, some months after her death from leukaemia. Muted colours and soft brush strokes take the edge off an almost too candid scene; yet the family involved fully approved, drawing strength from Susan's discreet presence. For Susan they were special people, made so through their experience of living with leukaemia. This particular painting is remarkable because she is able to provide the rest of us with a glimpse of this special quality. To contemplate it, evokes the innermost fears of the viewer, but the underlying message is one of continuity and hope – a modern-day mandala or symbol equivalent to those depicted on the ancient temples of Gigantija.

In 1998, Susan was one of 48 artists commissioned by the Royal Mail to design a postage stamp to mark the Millennium. The stamp was entitled *Nursing Care*, with a theme chosen to commemorate the work of Florence Nightingale in raising the status of nursing to that of a caring profession. Susan commented that the request by the Royal Mail was all 'rather unlikely' (she always played down her success), but here, unquestionably, was recognition.

Ronald G. Mackay, Captain RN

Captiva, Cannes

15

The Mackays at La Souche, Comps-sur-Artuby

Epilogue

Susan Macfarlane was fit, active and leading a very full life when, tragically, she died in August 2002 in an accident at home in Petersfield. She was 64. Ironically she had been preparing to open her studio to the public and, in contrast to the usual chaos, all was in order. Most striking among the various drawings and paintings intended for show were several large, unfinished oil scrubs of present-day life in South India, from where Susan had recently returned. It was to have been the beginning of a whole new phase. She would move to Tamil Nadu for three months in the year, perhaps for several years in succession. This would have enabled her to settle for a while, to make friends and contacts, and to gain the perspective necessary to produce original work.

Aside from her painting, the last few years had been good ones. Susan had moved to a new house (more manageable and with a purpose-built studio in the back garden), made new friends, seen both of her children married, and become a grandmother. The family had also transformed a three-acre field into a broadleaf woodland in the winter of 1997. Mac's Wood, as it has come to be known, shares a boundary with Susan's childhood home on Hampton Hill to one side and a family burial ground to the other, where her ashes are scattered together with those of her husband and parents.

One of the last major works that Susan completed was for Geoffrey Farrer-Brown's exhibition on the beauty of the blood supply to the heart. He had suggested to Susan that her topic might contain the theme of the universality of the Tree of Life, in nature and throughout time. The resulting painting, called *Dance of Life (A Celebration of Life)*, pp.110–11, is best described in her own words: 'Using a scroll pattern from prehistoric Maltese patterns to illustrate the renewal of life, I have superimposed Shiva as Nataraja, Lord of the Dance and source of all movements in the Universe. My work in Malta (Gozo), and more recently in South India, has invited this union of thought from two ancient cultures and confirms my own sense of overall continuity.'

Millennium stamp, March 1999

Tree of Life, Gozo

Susan at Mac's Wood, July 2002

Studio at 17 College Street, Petersfield, Hampshire

18 At her easel in Ceylon

On the quay in Hydra, Greece

The stone table at La Souche

At work in her studio, Petersfield

Susan Macfarlane – her work
by Alan Caiger-Smith

One day in March 2001 Susan and I were at the opening of a large exhibition in Christ Church, Spitalfields, in London. The exhibits included a wide range of objects in wood, glass, fabrics and clay, as well as paintings and drawings, all connected with the theme of art and health. Susan was showing three or four paintings relating to blindness, while I was represented by a group of large pots with thematic designs. A well-known critic had been invited, a pleasant man and a serious and enjoyable writer, whom I was looking forward to meeting. We were both introduced to him. After discussing my work he shook Susan's hand, glanced at her paintings and rather rapidly turned aside to speak to someone else. The discourtesy was probably not intended but it slightly surprised me. Susan, however, was dismayed. 'You see,' she said, 'I'm too descriptive. He's written me off.'

I was surprised that his lack of interest disconcerted her so much. After all, he was only a commentator, whereas she was a maker in the full flow of a phase of creative work, and had recently held a major exhibition at the Barbican. I never thought that a minor incident such as this could matter to her. Afterwards we had lunch together at a pub and I tried to put it in perspective, but she was distinctly aggrieved.

Susan's reaction was, in fact, understandable. She became a full-time painter in her early twenties and, though her subsequent marriage and the care of her family naturally limited the hours she could devote to painting in the middle phase of her life, her work maintained a definite continuity throughout. She was a professional; acknowledgement mattered. All artists, whatever their medium – be it paint or stone, words,

theatre or music – put an immense amount of experience, time and energy into what they do. The response, in the form of delight, applause or informed appreciation, returns some of that energy to the artist and helps them on. It is not a matter of ego but a circulation of energy: it goes out, it is exposed, and it is then returned to its source. In this case, the return flow had been stopped off and Susan was left adrift.

Possibly the response mattered all the more to her because, being a figurative painter, she felt that her work was being dismissed as merely representational, without any acknowledgement of its true content. She needn't have had any such misgivings: her originality was beyond question. She had immense creative energy and she produced an extensive body of work that transcended the ebb and flow of fashion in contemporary art. Susan attended art school only when she was very young, which may have been just as well. Had she continued, she could well have been set back, as were many of her contemporaries, by the variety of conflicting attitudes to art at the time. As things turned out, her life experience provided a richer grounding than she could have gained in any college environment. There was an uncanny rightness about the sequence of her life. Her travels and her meetings with people might be seen as matters of chance, but in hindsight they seem to have been more than providential. Stage by stage they drew her on to follow a path that was hers alone.

Susan had a broad appreciation of the history of art and was well informed about the various artistic outlooks that beset or enlivened the contemporary scene. She was not a modernist, but she was glad to absorb new ideas and techniques when they were on her wavelength and she could keep an open mind even when they were very different. Some of the discussions that mattered most to her were with the painter Frank Avray Wilson, whom she greatly respected. His book (*Art as Revelation*, 1981) and his philosophy of art, science and perception were of absorbing interest, even though his elemental expressionist paintings were poles apart from her own. Avray Wilson's ideas undoubtedly affected Susan's general outlook, though it is hard to discern any specific influence from them in her work.

Art is often described as a kind of communication. I don't think Susan thought much about communication: her work was first and foremost a response: communication would take care of itself. Indeed, the vividness of her work and the clarity of her ideas make her paintings naturally communicative. Increasingly, as time went by, her response to places and people evoked contingent memories and enriched the significance of what she saw. So it is for us today, who see the works she has left in her wake.

War Office cartoons 1958

As a child Susan loved animals and she drew them remarkably well. The same could be said of many children, yet to be able to draw is one thing, to *know* that you can draw is another. David Pare gave Susan this confirmation by giving her a place at the Winchester School of Art at the early age of 16 and she never forgot him. The assurance he gave her shows in the War Office cartoons (two of which are illustrated on page 22). Cartoons of well-known people are a kind of baptism by fire: everyone can judge their aptness and express an opinion. Susan's confident contours and her humorous observation of pose and character show her well able to take the risk, and to do so without belittling her subjects. Had she wished, she could have made a name for herself in this field but it seems that she deliberately passed it by.

Ceylon and East Asia 1960–62

In the East Susan found a new world of forms and colours, and a pattern of life which could hardly be dreamed of in England. *Dustbins, Ceylon*, p.33, might be seen as a version of the 'kitchen-sink' approach prevailing in London at that time, but its mood is very different because of the inclusion of a waiting child and the gang of crows investigating the human detritus. Susan made a large number of fairly rapid sketches of places she visited and people she met in the course of her active social life (for example, *Family Afloat*, p.33), but the carefully organized *Pettah Scene*, pp.30–31, is a total response to a world that was new to her. The lightly clothed dark limbs, the animals, birds and fruits evoke the interaction of humanity and the natural world of the tropics. Among a number of portraits painted in the East are *The Blue Jersey*, p.28 and *The Yellow Saree*, p.32, each of them about as different as could be from the War Office cartoons.

Greece 1963

Susan's sojourn in Greece on the way home was an opportunity to absorb something of a country she knew of only by hearsay, and to enjoy a period of informal apprenticeship with the painter John Dragoumis. Her immense output of drawings and paintings can only have been achieved by working intensively day by day to a planned programme, probably spurred on by Dragoumis's advice. She made studies of architecture and of sculptures, bronzes and pottery in museum collections, as well as sketching mountainsides, townscapes, hard-working donkeys, fishing boats and harbour scenes, and the activities of the local community. The buildings and their environment obviously delighted Susan, but she could not convey them adequately without including the life that went on in and around them. Her Greek sketches were instinctive, youthful responses to what she saw, but the places-and-people theme struck a deep chord within her. In the years ahead it was to develop into some major works, in ways she could not have foreseen.

In Greece Susan opened herself up to everything, and the range of the resulting drawings is remarkable. Among them are some perceptive studies of ancient Greek figure sculptures in stone and bronze, drawn with a searching line very different from the way she drew in the open air. In certain studies of carved heads Susan evidently found that her usual method of drawing in line and profile was inappropriate, and she turned instead to recording the forms solely in light and shade. These are more than intelligent artistic exercises: they are also evocations of the ancient world. Susan was evidently delighted also by the pottery – both the decorated vessels and the plain, swelling forms with their anthropomorphic implications. In one light-hearted drawing, which she entitled *Ancient Greek Gossip*, p.39, the pots seem to be talking to each other, like people in a market.

Something important and unexpected happened to Susan in Greece. The experience is best described in the words of her friend and mentor William Burman, to whom she had promised a painting:

'As the time for her departure drew near, Sue began to raise the subject of "my" painting, questioning me about the sort of thing I had in mind. In fact I had no preconceptions other than that I wanted a fairly large canvas that could be the sole feature of the living room created by the recent renovations. For a while I heard no more; and then one day she announced that she had a "cartoon" that she wanted me to see before she went any further with it. When I saw it, I knew at once that it wasn't right, but how was I to break this to her without hurting her feelings? What she had sketched was a hot, dusty Greek village scene, full of bustle and commotion, which was quite the antithesis of the sense of coolness and repose I had hoped for. I need not have worried. As soon as I began cautiously to explain

my feelings Sue grasped the point, agreeing with me and already moving on to new possibilities. All I remember is saying: "What about the sea, rock shapes, something of that sort?" Nothing more was said for a few days, but I was aware that Sue was leaving the house in the cool of the early morning, sailing a few miles along the coast with Michaelis the boatman, and returning to her studio a few hours later. Whenever I saw her she seemed confident, and absorbed in what she was doing. Finally she said: "I think I've solved it." There were no more tentative experiments, no more "cartoons". She had quietly given birth to what became known as *The Rocks*, something which for her proved to be a seminal work, and which for me and for many others has been a painting of lasting depth and beauty.'

The experience lifted Susan beyond her usual responses into a new realm. It took her into the contemplation of the virtually abstract structure of rocks. This in turn seems to have led her to review the structure of her compositions and indeed to think and to 'see' in ways that were quite new to her. This discovery, and the gradual reappraisal of herself, can be seen in a number of rock studies she made on the way to completing William Burman's large and wonderful painting. For many painters the massive forms of rocks, with their textures and colorations, have been sufficient formal inspiration in themselves to generate a long sequence of work. For Susan there was a further dimension – the virtual timelessness of the rocks, and their enduring presence behind the comings and goings of human beings, animals and all man-made things. Burman had intuitively led her to discover a wider frame, within which everything she had hitherto depicted took its place. She had grown, not only as an artist but also as a person. This dual awareness underlies a great deal of the work she did from this point onward, whatever the subject matter. It incorporates a sense of the ebb and flow of life on different scales, the time of the seasons, of human

21

NCCG.   Nov. 1958.   SHVH.   W.O. Nov' 1958

War Office cartoon I, 1958, Ink drawing, Family Collection   War Office cartoon II, 1958, Ink drawing, Family Collection

Saddled Mules, 1963, Ink drawing, Family Collection   Odeon of Herodes Atticus, 1962, Ink drawing, Family Collection

time and elemental time, and the traces they leave in the world around us.

Cannes 1964–75

The breakthrough brought about by *The Rocks*, p.41 enabled Susan to tackle what could otherwise have been a very problematic commission – the design of stained-glass windows for the Anglican church in Cannes. Not only did the task require an understanding of glass techniques and structure, but it was essentially conceptual and symbolic rather than being based on the direct, visual responses from which Susan normally worked. Her talk about working in glass, for which she wrote a script, is recorded in full on pages 125–29. 'The experience,' she said, 'was a bit of everything, as you may imagine – exciting, absorbing, terrifying, disappointing, and so on…' The talk is a wonderfully lucid blow-by-blow account of the process, delivered with typical verve. Reading between the lines, it also reveals a good deal about Susan herself.

She laid out the themes in careful drawings, and converted some of these into paintings before translating them into glass with the assistance of the master glazier Alain Peinado. The rock studies stood her in good stead. The panels of glass are disposed like a two-dimensional version of a rock-face, and the composition is held together by structural lines of force. The figurative themes are unified by a strong, abstract composition; some of the smaller windows are in fact entirely abstract. Designing for glass also made Susan think afresh about colour. Her natural response was linear: to use line to describe form and mass. When she intended to make a painting from a preparatory drawing she usually included notes as a guide to the colours and focal points of light and dark, but the colours were secondary to the drawing. Working with glass, she recognized that colour is a vital emotional key without which the mood of a work can never fully come across. Whereas her drawing was for the most part an on-the-spot response, her use of colours is evocative and

symbolical rather than literal: as in, for instance, the later Balblair painting *Rolling the Barrels*, p.89 and, from Gozo, *The High Altar – Sacrifice with Goats*, p.72. Years later, the experience of designing the stained-glass windows was to prove immensely valuable to her in planning the paintings of the Longford's Mill, the Balblair Distillery and the hospital subjects 'A Picture of Health' and 'Living with Leukaemia'.

Provence 1975–85

Figures of humans and animals – such a vital part of Susan's earlier work – seldom appear in her paintings and drawings from this period. In the introduction to a retrospective exhibition at the British Council in Brussels in March 1980, William Burman wrote: 'Her paintings reflect not only the awesome impersonality of space and form, but seem to comment on Man's impermanence and the fragility of his struggle to shape the physical world. That world, though stronger than Man, is also inseparable from him, and the absence of the human form in most of Susan Macfarlane's paintings, paradoxically enough, makes us more, not less, aware of this. Certainly, the artist's intensely human sense of solitude and pathos is everywhere apparent (the solitary tree, the abandoned, time-ravaged artefact) and we are made aware of something entirely personal and keenly felt.'

Family life and Susan's fairly secluded homes in Provence and Wiltshire kept the world of human activity at a distance. The life around her was written in the bodies of hills and mountains, plants, birds and animals. The earlier studies of rock formations are remembered, but now most often in the form of mountains dominating a landscape. Her landscapes could hardly be more different from the conventional genre of descriptive topographical paintings. There is always a guiding theme behind them, sometimes suggested by standing stones, as in the Avebury paintings, or by a mountainside, or by the unexpected

23

juxtaposition of particular features (*La Pierre de la Fée et sa Maison*, p.55 and *The Swift*, p.54). Visually they are very powerful, but Susan also thought deeply about the significance of what she was portraying. Frequently the paintings of this period indicate a wider world than the eye can see. Some of them are also, by deliberate implication, about time (for instance *Chestnut Buds*, p.52 and *Blue Hillside*, pp.50–51). They are indeed 'keenly felt' but they are not, in my view, 'entirely personal' – and certainly not in their impact. Rather, one has the sense of being shown something one had known all along but never fully recognized.

Two extraordinary seascapes, even though one of them is later in date, belong to the mood of this range of paintings: *Adriatic*, p.58 and *River Arun meets Incoming Tide*, pp.60–61. Susan did not often paint the sea but these two very different paintings show how inspiring it could be for her. Later, in 1993, she worked on a series of seascapes in Cornwall; as a much-needed intermission after completing the first set of hospital pictures.

Gozo 1992

In Malta, Susan's visit to the archaeological digs near the town of Gigantija on the island of Gozo clearly had an overwhelming impact on her, and brought together many facets of her previous output and her intuitive thinking. She made numerous careful drawings of the general terrain, and of the details of the stone tombs, temples and megalithic monuments, as well as large drawings of the archaeological team at work on the excavations. The contrast between the monkey-like diggers with their trowels, kettles and kitbags and the silent, mysterious 6,000-year-old stone structures seems to have struck her as both poignant and comical. Judging by the colour notes, she considered converting one or two of these excavation drawings into large paintings, but it seems that she never did so.

Instead, she produced a series of paintings evoking the life of the people whose presence she felt all around her (*Servants of Ritual*, pp.74–75; *A Crowd with Goats*

approaches Gigantija*, p.76; *The High Altar – Sacrifice with Goats*, p.72; *The Potter's Garden*, p.79). For her, the people of long ago were not primarily interesting as objects of scientific investigation; the most important thing about them was that their hearts and minds were not separate from our own. One painting (*The Earth Goddess*, p.79) is about just this concept. It brings together a figure of the goddess, a group of ancient worshippers and the Tree of Life symbol, which had recently been discovered carved on one of the stones. Later she made it the subject of a painting in its own right (*Tree of Life, Gozo* p.17). The beauty and significance of this symbol struck her very deeply and she quite often referred to it in our conversations.

Later, Susan used the same symbol as an emblem for her 'A Picture of Health' paintings, and it dominates one of the paintings she completed on her return from southern India in 2002 (*Dance of Life [A Celebration of Life]*, pp.110–11). Geoffrey Farrer-Brown had asked her whether she could produce a painting showing that the Tree of Life is a timeless universal theme. Susan responded with this painting, which she called a mandala. She felt that it had a therapeutic influence and suggested that it might be used by hospital patients for quiet contemplation. She saw it as a symbol of continuity: of the cycles of time generating one another, and of the life-giving power of the natural world over and above and beyond the lives of its various creatures. She always painted the symbol in green.

Longford's Mill and Balblair Distillery 1989–96

Months of continuous work went into both of these two major groups of paintings. The Longford's Mill series was exhibited in Gloucestershire with considerable aplomb as a record of historic local industry, yet it is really something much more ambitious than a documentary. Susan's youthful drawings in Greece had demonstrated her sensitivity to the relationship between places and people's activities. By the time she worked in the woollen mills and the distillery, this awareness had acquired a much deeper insight. What are they really about? Not simply places of work or processes of manufacture, but places where human beings come to know themselves and the world more deeply through their engagement in skilled work, their endurance, the risks they take, and the way they meet a challenge.

Susan built up both groups of paintings systematically, beginning with rapid pencil sketches of people in action; then making large and carefully observed drawings of buildings, equipment and machinery; and finally producing a variety of possible compositions, with colour notes, in which everything was brought together. For instance, the sketchbooks contain three or four alternative compositions for *The Stills, Balblair Distillery*, p.87. Only then was she ready to embark on the paintings themselves.

The people and the equipment belong together and are described with equal weight. Sometimes the figures are little more than silhouettes against the machinery (*Man in Blue*, p.83 and *Mangle – Diptych I & II*, pp.84–85). The real subject is the relationship between them. An earlier drawing of a threshing machine, p.49, shows Susan's fascination with machinery. In the Mill and Distillery paintings she shows it brought into action by human expertise (*Stillman Watches*, p.89 and *Checking the Wash*, p.88). These paintings belong to a particular place and time but in a sense are as timeless as her Gozo paintings, in that they are describing people's engagement with the world and their awareness of their own presence. Somewhat apart from all the rest is a delightful, slightly humorous painting. No one is at work in *Spools of Wool*, p.80. The weird shapes Susan saw in the spinning mechanism look back, consciously or unconsciously, to the figures of the archaeologists on Gozo, and they reappear later in her animated street scenes of Tamil Nadu.

'A Picture of Health' and 'Living with Leukaemia' *1992–97*

One thing leads to another. The Longford's Mill paintings were seen by the prominent histopathologist Dr Geoffrey Farrer-Brown, who

wrote: 'I was intrigued as to how an artist could portray such a drab working environment in oil paintings that were obviously highly acclaimed.' Farrer-Brown invited Susan to portray the work of a medical laboratory, resulting in nine pictures which impressed him so much that he was determined to follow up the project. This collaboration led to two extensive groups of paintings, totalling no fewer than 52 canvases: the first describing hospital care of breast cancer, the other on the subject of childhood leukaemia. A third series about blindness was considered, but only five of the subjects were ever finished. In due course Farrer-Brown, the dedicated promoter of the whole idea, arranged for the two completed series of paintings to be exhibited in some 40 different galleries and medical centres up and down the country, and in a number of venues in Ireland. A generously illustrated catalogue was published for each exhibition, with explanatory commentaries, including many of Susan's own observations. This major project is by far the most fully recorded of all her undertakings.

Susan was always a tireless worker. The medical paintings extended her more than anything she had ever produced before, and she devoted over five years to these projects. She spent months in hospitals and laboratories absorbing the significance of each aspect of the treatment, making sketches and notes before finally committing her impressions to canvas. In these paintings the theme of people and places, which had surfaced in various ways all through her career, took on a new dimension. In the Longford's Mill and Balblair Distillery paintings she had portrayed individual men and women in a kind of partnership with machinery; in these new paintings she had to describe not only the people and the locations, but also human relationships, the significance of the processes taking place and the response of the patients and their families.

The detail of the hospital paintings required careful thought. So also did the overall compositions, which often involved the inclusion of a number

25

of related figure studies as well as a description of the equipment and environment. To bring all this together Susan devised an unusual extended-perspective structure, based on curving rather than straight lines of recession, comparable to a wide-angled lens (*First Day of the Future*, p.97). This was a breakthrough: it enabled her to convey what was taking place without being distracted by literal detail, and allowed her to bring together several different aspects of an event within one canvas (as in *Radiotherapy*, p.102 and *Typing the Leukaemic Cells*, p.98). It also gave each picture an extraordinary emotional force, a sense of suspended time, as if the whole world were at that moment concentrated in a single event in one particular place (for instance *Theatre III*, p.93 and *A Moment of Beauty*, p.94).

'Other paintings in the series bring together the technology of the treatment and the medical skills required to apply it (as in *Checking the Slides I*, p.96). In describing the interaction of people and equipment she drew upon her former work at the woollen mills and distillery, but the entire mood of the medical paintings is of course very different.

A patient commented: 'The public should be better informed about cancer. These paintings reach out to dispel some of the fear.' In art, they are a virtually unique achievement. Behind and within them is the realization that some of the most traumatic events in life cannot be tackled by evasion, only by being embraced in total and in detail. Some members of the public were deterred from seeing these exhibitions because they dealt with fear, pain and suffering. That was a pity, because they were every bit as much about courage, dedication and freedom.

Contemporary art frequently concentrates on horror and pain. It is at times deliberately confrontational, seeking to show the unpalatable 'reality' of things by shock tactics. Sometimes this is not much more than an adopted attitude with little real feeling behind it – a way of forcing a public response by storm. The hospital paintings are something totally different. They look fair and square at certain aspects of human suffering and fear, and by doing so they see beyond them. There are no holds barred, but the paintings are also deeply compassionate. *After Alice*, p.105, in the leukaemia series is an example. Again, the painting is partly about time. Susan once pointed out to me that the clock is a key feature: a small child's time has stopped, but her family must go on living by its measure.

The medical paintings had to be true to Susan's own experience; she never strove to impress. As Elizabeth Gledhill wrote in one of the reviews of the exhibition: 'The artist stresses the importance of remaining an observer... She abhors vehemently the idea of trying to "do good" by her art. She remains concerned only with her paintings and not with what the public thinks of them.' These paintings are an artistic achievement of a high order and they are also a profoundly positive record of humanity.

A national acknowledgement of Susan's achievement was the commission in 1998 to produce a painting for a Millennium postage stamp. The finished stamp was entitled *Nursing Care*, p.17, commemorating the work of Florence Nightingale. The commission was a small tribute compared with all Susan had done, but characteristically she regarded it as a great honour.

Southern India 2002

Susan returned to the East in January 2002. This time she went not to Sri Lanka, where her painting career had taken off, but to Tamil Nadu in southern India. She was fulfilling a plan that had been taking shape in her mind for several years and, as with many other events in her life, there was an extraordinary rightness about it.

Her response to India was first and foremost a visual one – the people, the animals, the beautiful Brahmin bulls (*Brahmin Bulls*, p.106), buildings, bicycles, movement and colour (*The Purple Saree*, p.112). However, there was a great deal more to it. Her responses followed up not only the recurring themes that inspired her all through her life, but also people's dealings with each other and with animals, and, once again Time – the flow of daily life in relation to an enduring background. The background now was not rocks or mountainsides but the stone structures of massive Hindu temples and the stonework of their walls, carved long ago with scenes of humans and animals, and with figures of deities incarnating elemental forces.

Her idea was to spend three months in India each winter filling her sketchbooks with first-hand impressions, and then to develop them into paintings in her new studio in Petersfield during the rest of the year. This was her normal way of working; after the early days in the East she seldom painted directly from life.

The resulting sketchbooks contain numerous large, detailed versions of street scenes, bazaars, temple festivals and places of work, as usual accompanied by colour notes. She occasionally added evocative comments, as in the sketches of the market at Chennai (pp.108–9): 'This was where I had to draw those who stood around me, including a large priest with white beard and heavy forehead markings – very jolly!' Beside another sketch are some revealing words which could be applied to much of her work, but which belong especially to her time in India. 'Not myself, but where I am and what that is! More, to put what was there through me.' Two paintings, both untitled and apparently unfinished, show the process of putting 'what was there through me' in action (*Southern Indian Colours*, p.116 and *Orange Indian Figures*, p.117). These pictures are all the more telling because, as they

are unfinished, we ourselves are – so to speak – invited into them, to complete them in our imagination.

Most memorable of all the India paintings, however, is the *Dance of Life (A Celebration of Life)*, p.110–11, which Susan worked on immediately after her return to England and which is rather different from anything else she ever did. The figure of the dancing Nataraja, the sacred embodiment of the universal life force, flanked by two smaller figures, is represented within the green spirals of the ancient symbol she had seen in Gozo. The painting evokes the movement of life in passing time as part of a timeless process.

There is no reason to suppose that Susan had any premonition of her untimely, accidental death, but, if her time had to come to an end on that fateful day, then this work is the most perfect summing up of her thought and experience, and her love of life in all its forms.

After looking at paintings, people often find that they see the supposedly familiar world in a new way. They are surprised by seeing it as the painter might have seen it, rather than in the way they are accustomed to. Colours and shapes are perceived differently; the figures and features of the world take on a fresh significance. This is a painting's mysterious 'second wind'. It means that the painter's work is not restricted to the colours applied to a physical canvas, but extends into the mind and perception of the viewer: it is the painter's final and most lasting gift. In this sense Susan's work becomes part of the life of all those who have been fortunate enough to know it, and of those who will do so in years to come.

27

Alan Caiger-Smith MBE. Born Buenos Aires 1930. Foundation Scholar in History, King's College, Cambridge 1949–52; Student of Ceramics, Central School, London 1954–55. Established and directed Aldermaston Pottery 1955–93. Chairman, British Crafts Centre 1974–78. Publications: *Medieval English Mural Paintings*, Clarendon Press 1964; *Tin Glaze Pottery*, Faber 1973; *Piccolpasso's Three Books of the Potter's Art*, Scolar Press 1980 (co-editor with Ronald Lightbrown); *Lustre Pottery*, Faber 1985; Pottery, *People and Time*, Richard Dennis Publications 1995.

28

1 The Blue Jersey

Ceylon, East Asia and Greece 1960–63

The paintings and drawings in this section are a selection of the work Susan did when first living outside England; it was a period where she responded at random to whatever caught her fancy. She had a job and a full social life and, like other travellers before her, drew and painted whenever she got the chance. However, she was beginning to recognize that, whatever else happened, she must sooner or later become a full-time painter.

During her prolonged stay in Greece, Susan put her decision to the test, making a large number of studies of buildings, popular life and antiquities, and working to an intensive, self-imposed programme. Towards the end of her stay came a breakthrough: the commission to paint The Rocks.

2 Pettah Scene

3 The Yellow Saree

4 Dustbins, Ceylon

5 Family Afloat

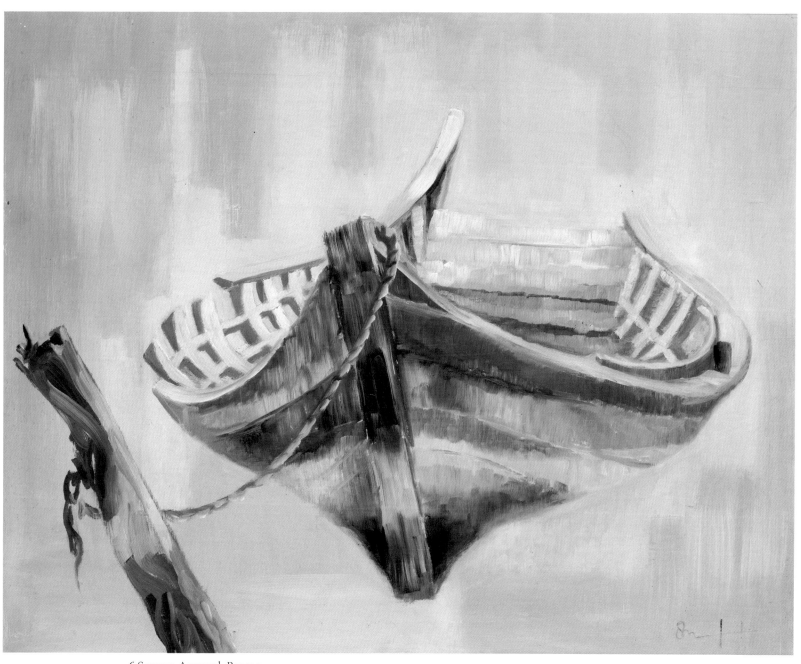

6 Sampan Aground, Penang

7 Hydra, View of the Port

ΥΔΡΑ
HYDRA.

8 Hydra I

9 Patras Fishermen

10 'To dine', Yapa

11 The Propylea from inside the Acropolis

12 The Jockey

13 Ancient Greek God

"ANCIENT
GREEK
GOSSIP"

FROM 8" to 10"
HIGH.

14 Ancient Greek Gossip

39

THE PROPYLAEA
FROM INSIDE THE ACROPOLIS
10·9·62.

40   *15* Hydra

16 The Rocks

17 Gorge de L'Artuby

Cannes, Provence and Wiltshire 1964–85

By now Susan was married with two small sons, but it was clear that she was a full-time painter and her work began to develop. The initial obvious impression of a subject now became simply the starting point for a deeper response. The major commission for stained-glass windows for the Anglican church in Cannes proved, unexpectedly, to be a vital stage in her professional self-assurance.

Later on, landscapes predominate, reflecting the secluded pattern of Susan's family life, but they are more thoughtful than any established descriptive landscape convention. They are just as much about scales of time, conveyed by the juxtaposition of objects with a long or a short life-span.

44

18 Blue Rocks

19 Orange Rocks

20 Parable I, Old Testament

21 Parable II, Old Testament

46

22 Strip Farming – Poppies

23 Vallauris, La Place

24 Esterelle

25 As it was in the beginning, is now…

26 Threshing Machine

50

27 Blue Hillside

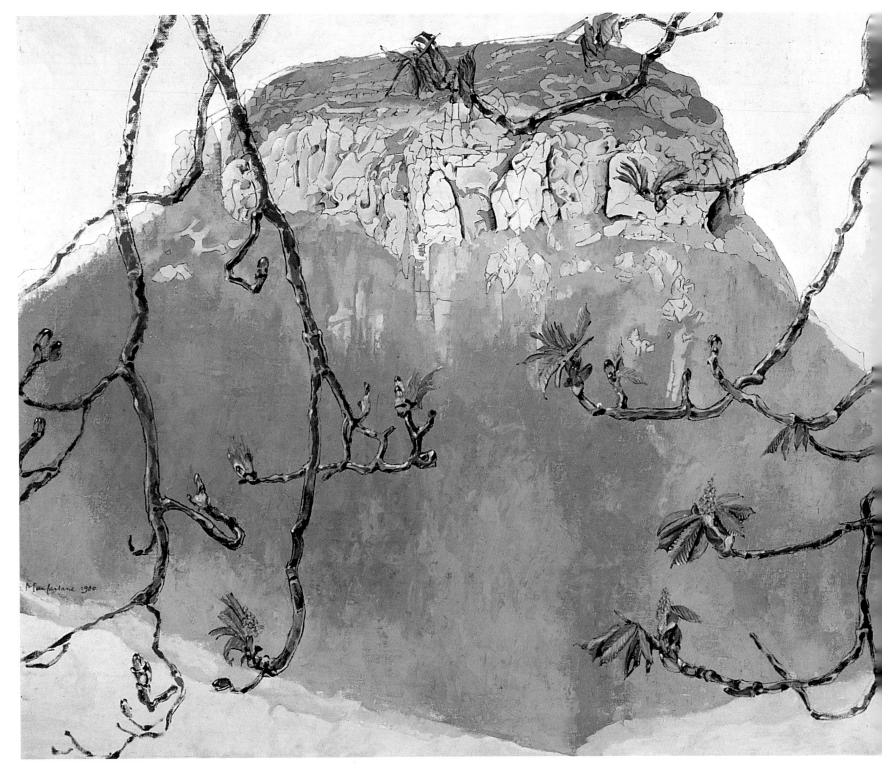

28 Chestnut Buds

29 The Ridge

53

30 The Tree – Space, Mass and Evolution

54

31 The Swift

32 Great Tit – Aggression

33 La Pierre de la Fée et sa Maison

34 Children among the Sarsen Stones

35 Adriatic

Occasional paintings 1981–2002

These paintings originate from various places, and in some cases the dates are uncertain. Some, like the extraordinary River Arun meets Incoming Tide *and other sea paintings, were prompted by a single vivid experience; others reflect in various ways Susan's awareness of the bond between human beings, both past and present, and of the environment that nurtures them.*

36 'Capricorn' makes Waves

37 River Arun meets Incoming Tide

38 Poseidon and the Blue-maned Horse

39 Portrait with Leaves

40 Brood Mares

41 The Shandwick Stone

42 The Nigg Pictish Stone

43 Mombasa Fishermen, Kenya

44 Sketch I, Kenya

45 Sketch II, Kenya

46 Masai Warrior, Kenya

47 The High Altar – Sacrifice with Goats

Gozo *1991–92*

Working on Gozo was an overwhelming experience. Almost everyone is aware of unseen

presences within and around ancient monuments, and here, for Susan, the seen and

the unseen were inseparable. The paintings in this section pay tribute to the builders

of a forgotten civilization, yet are rooted in the present.

73

48 Servants of Ritual

49 A Crowd with Goats approaches Gigantija

50 Past and Present

52 Gigantija, North Temple

51 Archaeological Dig I, Gozo

53 Spiral Motif and Fireplace

54 The Potter's Garden

55 The Earth Goddess

56 Spools of Wool

Longford's Mill and Balblair Distillery 1989–96

Both these series of paintings began as a record of manufacturing processes, and Susan spent a considerable amount of time making preparatory sketches in the two factories. The experience grew on her, and the 'documentary' drawings acquired a dimension beyond anything she or her sponsors had expected.

57 The Cutting Machine

58 Man in Blue

59 Mangle – Diptych I

60 Mangle – Diptych II

61 Ghosts of the Millhouse

62 The Stills, Balblair Distillery

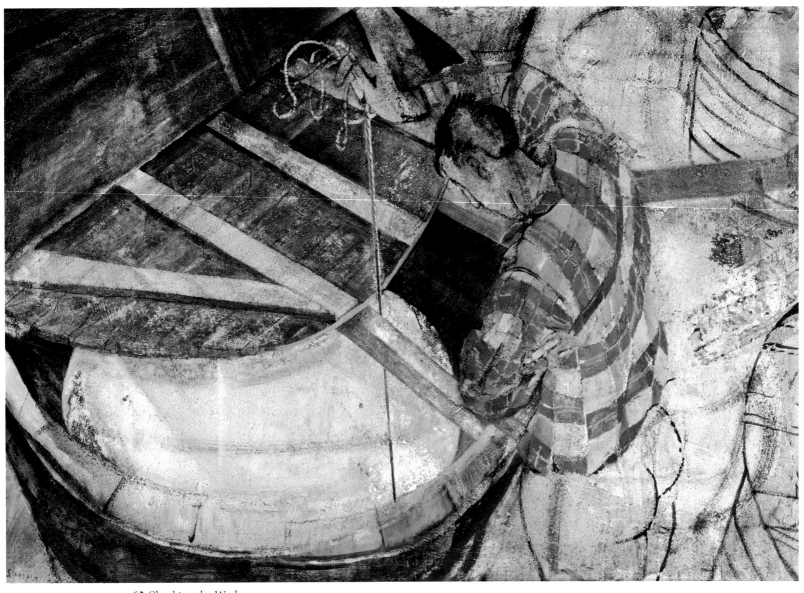

63 Checking the Wash

64 Stillman Watches

65 Rolling the Barrels

66 The Waiting Room

'A Picture of Health' 1992–94

This is the first of two extensive series of paintings representing a partnership between two highly original minds. Dr Farrer-Brown persuaded Susan into a project that stretched her ingenuity, and which few other artists could or would have taken on. The result is a unique record of 20th-century medical skills in action.

91

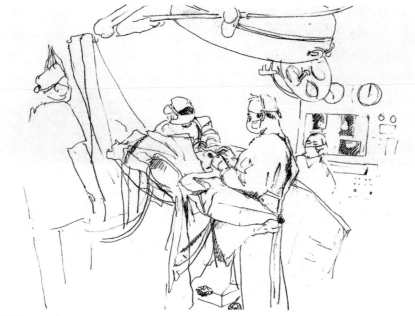

67 Theatre I

68 Theatre II

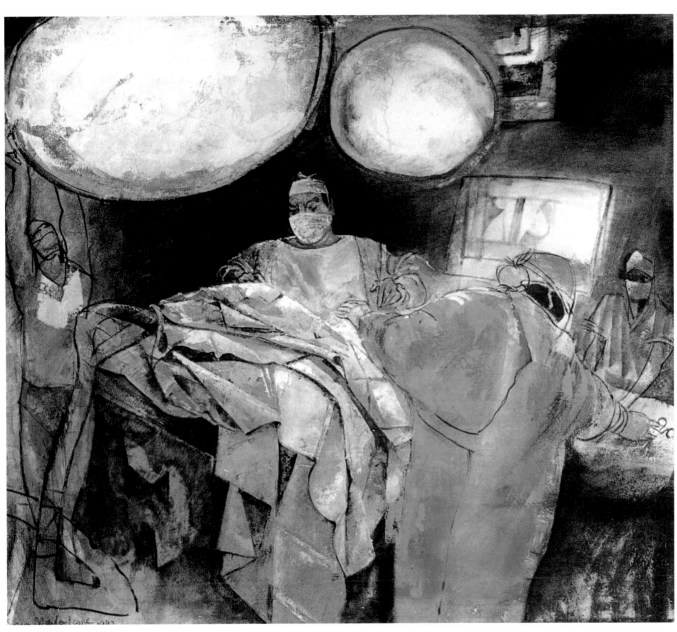

69 Theatre III

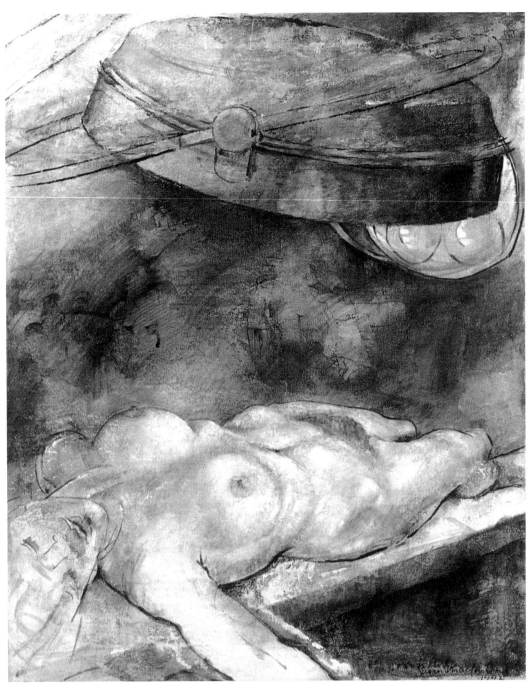

70 A Moment of Beauty

71 Recovery III

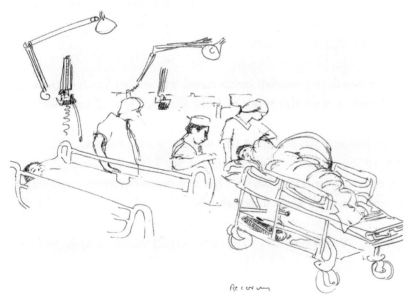

72 Recovery I

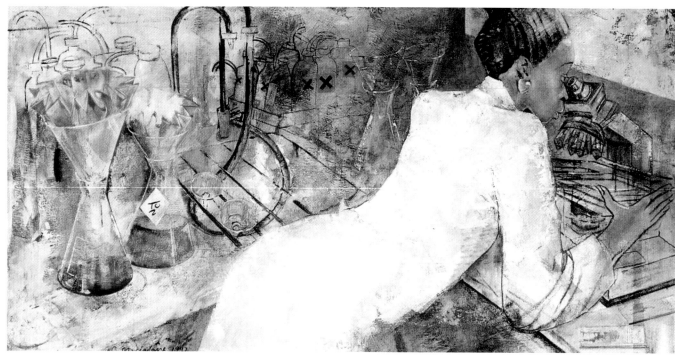

73 Checking the Slides I

74 Staining of Sections II

75 First Day of the Future

76 Typing the Leukaemic Cells

'Living with Leukaemia' 1996–97

This series developed intuitively, rather than to a preordained programme. Perhaps

because they concern children, the leukaemia paintings describe the psychological

as much as the physical aspects of treatment.

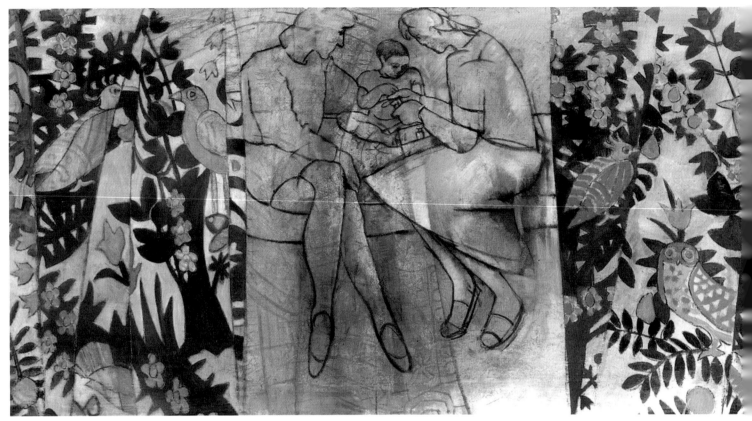

77 The Hickman Line

100

78 Sleeping it Off

79 Radiotherapy

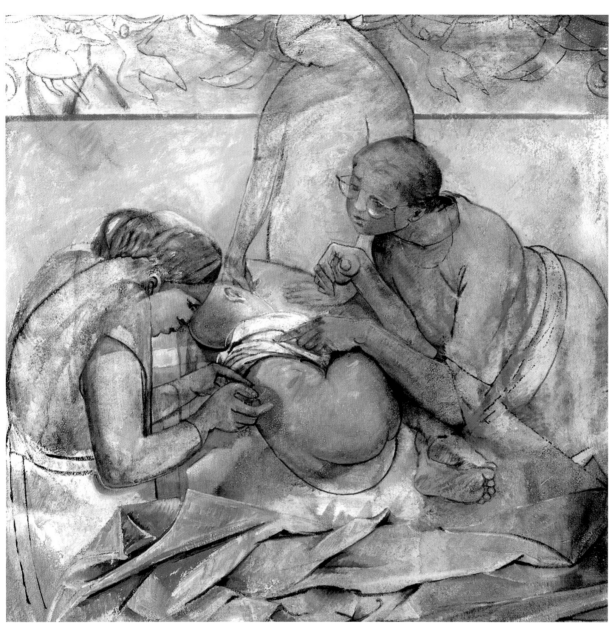

80 Lumbar Puncture

81 Curiosity

82 After Alice

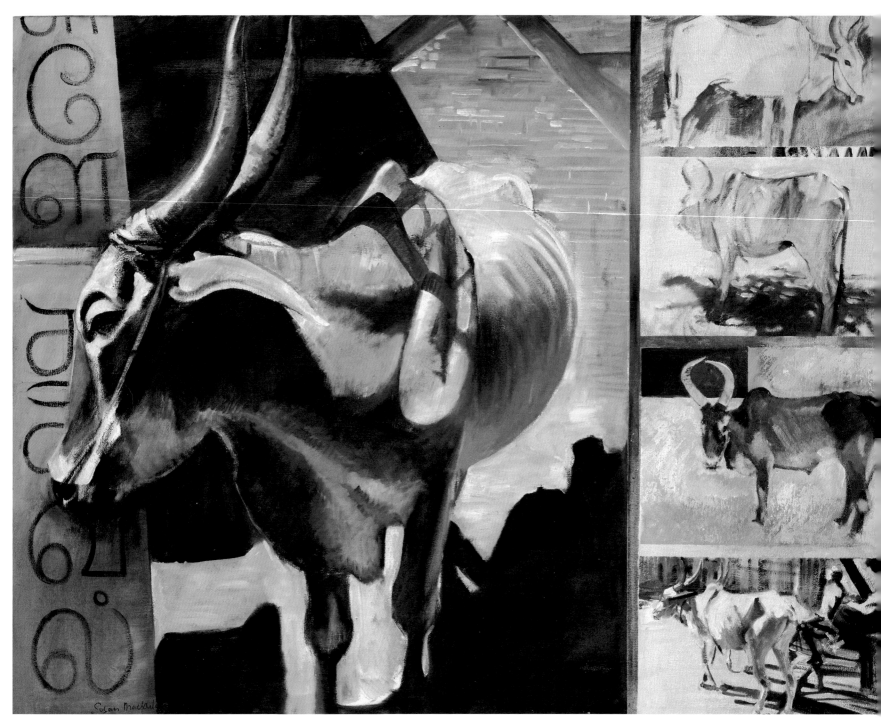

83 Brahmin Bulls

Southern India 2002

These paintings form the tantalizing beginning of a project, which Susan had planned for some time and did not live to fulfil. As she herself wrote: 'Not myself, but where I am and what that is! More, to put what was there through me.'

Chennai

Buffalo

84 Buffalo and Calves, Chennai

Chennai. Mylapore Market.
This was where I had to draw those who stood around me
including a huge priest with white beard & heavy forehead markings a very jolly P.

85 Mulapore Market

86 Market Scene, Chennai

87 Tangore

88 Dance of Life (A Celebration of Life)

89 The Purple Saree

90 The Apprentice

91 The Paper Mill, Southern India

92 Southern Indian Colours

93 Orange Indian Figures

118

List of plates

1
The Blue Jersey
1961
Oil on wood
63 x 47 cm
Private Collection

2
Pettah Scene
1961
Oil on wood
29 x 64 cm
Private Collection

3
The Yellow Saree
1961
Oil on wood
15 x 12 cm
Private Collection

4
Dustbins, Ceylon
1961
Oil on wood
29 x 75 cm
Family Collection

5
Family Afloat
1961
Oil on wood
29 x 64 cm
Private Collection

6
Sampan Aground, Penang
1962
Oil on wood
59 x 74 cm
Private Collection

7
Hydra, View of the Port
1962
Oil on canvas
66 x 76 cm
Private Collection

8
Hydra I
1962
Ink drawing
36 x 27 cm
Family Collection

9
Patras Fishermen
1962
Ink drawing
26 x 36 cm
Family Collection

10
'To dine', Yapa
1962
Ink drawing
40 x 29 cm
Family Collection

11
The Propylea from inside
the Acropolis
1962
Ink drawing
26 x 36 cm
Family Collection

12
The Jockey
1962
Ink drawing
17 x 18 cm
Family Collection

13
Ancient Greek God
1962
Pencil drawing
20 x 17 cm
Family Collection

14
Ancient Greek Gossip
1962
Ink drawing
13 x 22 cm
Family Collection

15
Hydra
1963
Oil on canvas
47 x 68 cm
Family Collection

16
The Rocks
1963
Oil on canvas
200 x 175 cm
Private Collection

17
Gorge de L'Artuby
1975
Oil on canvas
122 x 61 cm
Private Collection

18
Blue Rocks
1973
Dalles de verre et resine
400 x 100 cm
Cannes, Holy Trinity

19
Orange Rocks
1973
Dalles de verre et resine
400 x 100 cm
Cannes, Holy Trinity

20
Parable I, Old Testament
1976
Stained glass (Grisaille)
100 x 250 cm
Cannes, Holy Trinity

21
Parable II, Old Testament
1976
Stained glass (Grisaille)
100 x 250 cm
Cannes, Holy Trinity

22
Strip Farming – Poppies
1980
Oil on canvas
70 x 34 cm
Private Collection

23
Vallauris, La Place
1967
Oil on canvas
24 x 28 cm
Private Collection

24
Esterelle
1965
Oil on canvas
62 x 135 cm
Family Collection

25
As it was in the beginning,
is now…
1977
Oil on canvas
31 x 52 cm
Private Collection

26
Threshing Machine
circa 1977
Pencil drawing
41 x 59 cm
Family Collection

27
Blue Hillside
1976
Oil on canvas
77 x 103 cm
Private Collection

28
Chestnut Buds
1980
Oil on canvas
33 x 41 cm
Private Collection

29
The Ridge
1980
Oil on canvas
29 x 41 cm
Private Collection

30
The Tree – Space,
Mass and Evolution
1977
Oil on canvas
70 x 84 cm
Private Collection

31
The Swift
1983
Oil on canvas
18 x 25 cm
Private Collection

32
Great Tit – Aggression
1983
Oil on canvas
15 x 29 cm
Private Collection

33
La Pierre de la Fée
et sa Maison
1982
Oil on canvas
70 x 110 cm
Family Collection

34
Children among
the Sarsen Stones
1987
Oil on canvas
69 x 122 cm
Family Collection

35
Adriatic
1981
Oil on canvas
64 x 74 cm
Private Collection

36
'Capricorn' makes Waves
circa 1993
Oil on canvas
66 x 66 cm
Family Collection

37
River Arun meets
Incoming Tide
1993
Oil on canvas
30 x 61 cm
Private Collection

38
Poseidon and the
Blue-maned Horse
1994
Oil on canvas
92 x 92 cm
Private Collection

39
Portrait with Leaves
1989
Oil on canvas
43 x 56 cm
Family Collection

40
Brood Mares
circa 1990
Oil on canvas
18 x 28 cm
Private Collection

41
The Shandwick Stone
2002
Oil on canvas
134 x 183 cm
Private Collection

42
The Nigg Pictish Stone
circa 2000
Oil on canvas
81 x 122 cm
Family Collection

43
Mombasa Fishermen, Kenya
2001
Oil on canvas
76 x 81 cm
Family Collection

44
Sketch I, Kenya
2001
Pencil drawing
13 x 29 cm
Family Collection

45
Sketch II, Kenya
2001
Pencil drawing
13 x 29 cm
Family Collection

46
Masai Warrior, Kenya
2001
Oil on canvas
77 x 92 cm
Family Collection

47
The High Altar –
Sacrifice with Goats
1992
Oil on canvas
66 x 76 cm
Family Collection

48
Servants of Ritual
1992
Oil on canvas
61 x 91 cm
Private Collection

49
A Crowd with Goats
approaches Gigantija
1992
Oil on canvas
54 x 30 cm
Family Collection

50
Past and Present
1992
Oil on canvas
20 x 66 cm
Family Collection

51
Archaeological Dig I, Gozo
1991
Pencil drawing
50 x 37 cm
Family Collection

52
Gigantija, North Temple
1991
Pencil drawing
50 x 37 cm
Family Collection

53
Spiral Motif and Fireplace
1992
Oil on canvas
61 x 61 cm
Family Collection

54
The Potter's Garden
1992
Oil on canvas
29 x 45 cm
Family Collection

55
The Earth Goddess
1992
Oil on canvas
35 x 25 cm
Family Collection

56
Spools of Wool
1989
Oil on canvas
29 x 45 cm
Family Collection

57
The Cutting Machine
1991
Oil on canvas
76 x 87 cm
Family Collection

58
Man in Blue
1991
Oil on canvas
60 x 54 cm
Family Collection

59
Mangle – Diptych I
1990
Oil on canvas
67 x 61 cm
Family Collection

60
Mangle – Diptych II
1990
Oil on canvas
67 x 61 cm
Family Collection

61
Ghosts of the Millhouse
1990
Oil on canvas
60 x 100 cm
Private Collection

62
The Stills, Balblair Distillery
1996
Oil on canvas
86 x 75 cm
Private Collection

63
Checking the Wash
1996
Oil on canvas
16 x 25 cm
Private Collection

64
Stillman Watches
1996
Oil on canvas
46 x 91 cm
Private Collection

65
Rolling the Barrels
1996
Oil on canvas
71 x 70 cm
Private Collection

66
The Waiting Room
1992
Oil on canvas
74 x 74 cm
Private Collection

67
Theatre I
1992
Pencil drawing
40 x 50 cm
Private Collection

68
Theatre II
1992
Pencil drawing
42 x 58 cm
Private Collection

69
Theatre III
1992
Oil on canvas
74 x 84 cm
Private Collection

70
A Moment of Beauty
1992
Oil on canvas
76 x 59 cm
Private Collection

71
Recovery III
1992
Oil on canvas
65 x 84 cm
Private Collection

72
Recovery I
1992
Pencil drawing
40 x 50 cm
Private Collection

73
Checking the Slides I
1992
Oil on canvas
46 x 86 cm
Private Collection

74
Staining of Sections II
1992
Oil on canvas
56 x 79 cm
Private Collection

75
First Day of the Future
1994
Oil on canvas
46 x 65 cm
Private Collection

76
Typing the Leukaemic Cells
1996
Oil on canvas
35 x 100 cm
Private Collection

77
The Hickman Line
1996
Oil on canvas
46 x 86 cm
Private Collection

78
Sleeping it Off
1996
Oil on canvas
66 x 76 cm
Private Collection

79
Radiotherapy
1996
Oil on canvas
78 x 88 cm
Private Collection

80
Lumbar Puncture
1996
Oil on canvas
74 x 74 cm
Private Collection

81
Curiosity
1996
Oil on canvas
46 x 56 cm
Private Collection

82
After Alice
1997
Oil on canvas
56 x 101 cm
Private Collection

83
Brahmin Bulls
2002
Oil on canvas
76 x 97 cm
Family Collection

84
Buffalo and Calves, Chennai
2002
Pencil drawing
15 x 20 cm
Family Collection

85
Mulapore Market
2002
Pencil drawing
29 x 41 cm
Family Collection

86
Market Scene, Chennai
2002
Pencil drawing
29 x 41 cm
Family Collection

87
Tangore
2002
Pencil drawing
29 x 41 cm
Family Collection

88
Dance of Life
(A Celebration of Life)
2002
Oil on canvas
45 x 85 cm
Private Collection

89
The Purple Saree
2002
Oil on canvas
76 x 71 cm
Family Collection

90
The Apprentice
2002
Oil on canvas
23 x 29 cm
Family Collection

91
The Paper Mill, Southern India
2002
Oil on canvas
66 x 91 cm
Family Collection

92
Southern Indian Colours
2002
Oil on canvas
76 x 90 cm
Family Collection

93
Orange Indian Figures
2002
Oil on canvas
90 x 76 cm
Family Collection

List of exhibitions

1960   Times of Ceylon Gallery, Colombo,
        Sri Lanka

1961   Galle Face, Colombo, Sri Lanka

1962   St John's Cathedral Old Hall, Hong Kong

1963   Guildhall, Winchester, UK

1972   Commissioned to design the stained
        glass for the new Holy Trinity Church,
        Cannes, France

1979   Corpus Christi College, Oxford, UK

        Patricia Wells Gallery, Bristol, UK

1980   Ash Barn Gallery, Petersfield, UK

        British Council Exhibition, Brussels, Belgium

1982   Archaeological Museum Gallery, Devizes, UK
        'Ancient Wiltshire'

1985   Arts Council Affiliated Exhibition,
        Leicester, UK

1991   Kreihaus Göttingen, Lower Saxony,
        Germany

1992   The Subscription Rooms, Stroud, UK
        'The Woollen Mills of Stroud –
        An Artist's Impression'

        Archaeological Museum Gallery, Devizes, UK
        'An Artist in Ancient Gozo'

1993   Royal College of Pathologists, London, UK
        'Medicine at Work'

1995   The Foyer Gallery, Barbican Centre,
        London, UK – 'A Picture of Health'

        'A Picture of Health' touring exhibition:
            Royal College of Surgeons, Edinburgh
            Bonington Gallery, Nottingham
            St David's Hall, Cardiff
            Manchester Museum
            Westgate Library, Oxford
            Birmingham Museum of Science
            Royal West of England Academy, Bristol

1996   Brown's Gallery, Tain, Ross-shire, UK
        'Balblair – A Working Distillery'

1998   The Foyer Gallery, Barbican Centre,
        London, UK – 'Living with Leukaemia'

        'Living with Leukaemia' touring exhibition:
            Gloucestershire Royal Hospital, Gloucester
            Musgrove Park Hospital, Taunton

2002   European Forum on the Arts in Hospitals
        and Healthcare, Strasbourg, France

Susan Macfarlane also exhibited regularly in mixed
exhibitions throughout her life, including the
annual open exhibition at the Royal West of England
Academy, Bristol, UK.

Media comment

'**A moment of beauty**' – Susan Macfarlane's style is a mixture of the modernism we associate with Ben Nicholson and the more direct approach of Stanley Spencer – a very English kind of painting. The paint is put on in a roughly textured ground which is built up by line and patches of colour to a point where the image is suggested enough to be recognized but not so much that the spontaneity of the impression is lost.

Malcolm Miles, British Healthcare Arts, October 1993

'**A testing time**' – Believing that art can play an important role in stimulating awareness of a subject on both an intellectual and emotional level, she has depicted intimate and deeply serious scenes in an accessible and very personal way.

Home & Country, October 1994

'**From clinic to gallery**' – Susan Macfarlane's oils and drawings derive from sketches she made in operating theatres. They bring a disconcerting beauty to their stark subject… About Miss Macfarlane's patients there is something courageous, while her doctors are silent, almost mechanical, figures.

The Daily Telegraph, January 1995

'**A portrait of breast cancer**' – Breast cancer care is an unlikely and unpromising subject for an artist, but in the series of 40 oil paintings and drawings… Susan Macfarlane has produced a moving record of hospital and laboratory scenes.

Philippa Ingram, The Times, February 1995

'**Self-conscious portraits**' – The simplicity, humour and nonsentimental directness of her approach gives her work an added force.

William Packer, Financial Times, March 1995

'**Pictures of health**' – Susan Macfarlane's drawings, and particularly her paintings, achieve an extraordinary balance between observation and sympathy. The comparison that comes immediately, if surprisingly, to mind is with war artists… She brings a pragmatic scepticism to the subject, a critical distance, which balances the inherent risk of sentimentality.

Rosemary Hill, Artists Newsletter, May 1995

'**True to life**' – Susan Macfarlane's paintings are of a world not often visited by artists: the children's leukaemia ward of a hospital. The pictures themselves… are an extraordinary reminder of life on a hospital ward, the little world closing in around the parent and the child.

Bibi van der Zee, The Guardian, March 1998

'**Strokes of genius in war on cancer**' – A series of remarkable paintings revealing the heartache and hope behind the treatment of cancer in children… a similar exhibition by the artist, on breast cancer, was highly acclaimed as proving that art can open up an enclosed world in an intensely moving way.

Manchester Evening News, April 1999

Other mentions include:

February–April 1992: coverage of Susan's drawings and paintings of the Woollen Mills of Stroud in *Homes & Gardens*, *Gloucestershire Life* and *Cotswold Life*.

February–March 1998: coverage of Susan's series of paintings, 'Living with Leukaemia', in the *Art Review*, *Women's Health*, *The Lancet*, *The Citizen* and the *Evening Post*.

Maquette I, Holy Trinity, 1975, Pencil drawing, 10 x 22 cm, Family Collection

Maquette II, Holy Trinity, 1975, Pencil drawing, 10 x 22 cm, Family Collection

A commission for stained glass
Susan's talk about her work at Holy Trinity Church, Cannes

I have hoped that the title for this talk, 'A commission for stained glass', will have given you the clue to my status: not a master glazier but simply a painter rash enough to take on a commission for designs for stained-glass windows. However, in order to carry the thing off I did have to learn quite a lot about the techniques, and quite fast. The experience was a bit of everything as you may imagine, exciting, absorbing, terrifying, disappointing and so on, but it did occur to me that the tale of a complete stranger to the craft might be worth telling in the hope that some understanding of the methods involved, some of the do's and don'ts, might enhance your appreciation, like mine, when visiting the many wonderful cathedrals and churches; for in fact the techniques have changed very little over the centuries. Should there be a real master glazier in the house then he will surely learn little from me except perhaps to know how important he is to the uninitiated artist dragged into the game with a commission!

The whole thing began for me while living near Cannes in the south of France with my husband and two small boys. A new Anglican church was to be built on the site of a very dilapidated Victorian one on hallowed ground in perpetuity, both in the eyes of God and incidentally those of the local building promoter, since the site is just behind the Carlton Hotel. In order to have some Anglican say in the design a rather smart British church architect from Lambeth Palace was sent out to oversee the local architect's plans and to 'see us right', so to speak. Anyhow this nice man came to have a drink with my husband one morning, I'm not sure why, and he saw

my paintings hanging around – you know how it is. Well, he thought, it would be a great plan if I should tender designs for the so far unplanned windows, and I have to say I was very doubtful indeed – for how could one know what to do – even to start?

However, plans were produced and it all seemed worse and worse, for the area to be filled with glass seemed to grow and grow. First they talked of a strip right across the west end of the church, high above the altar facing east; you know, one of those where the priest faces you. This bit was merely 11 metres wide and 1 metre high, but then they added two lobes, floor-to-ceiling jobs on either side so that the poor fellow was going to be kind of entombed in glass! Well, we did eventually produce these windows but I'm not going to tell you about them because they are made in *dalles de verre* set in epoxy resin, and it is nothing like as interesting to learn about as antique glass in lead. *Dalles de verre* is really used for modern concrete buildings, such as Coventry Cathedral and incidentally the R.C. one here in Bristol and indeed this new Holy Trinity Church in Cannes.

We found a secondhand copy of Patrick Reyntiens's out-of-print book entitled *The Technique of Stained Glass* and I was introduced to a charming master glazier who seemed willing to work with a complete innocent. The book became my Bible and the glazier, if not God, then a Guru and guardian.

The windows that I *do* want to tell you about were to be made in antique glass set in lead, entirely traditional, using all the ancient techniques used for the earliest samples of stained glass – although certain things are much easier today (for example, a thermostat in the kilns for firing to the correct temperature, and also a far greater choice of colours – some 600 opportunities when I was involved, but that can really be a disadvantage I think!) – Quote from Old Testament texts. Heavens what a chance! – But it still had to be done.

So away I went with P.R. and I must say his book is quite remarkable. If you could learn a craft from a book then this is the one that can teach you: everything you could need to the last possibility, even how to build your studio.

For me the first pearl to be dropped was 'first paint a picture'. This may seem obvious but the advice proved of enormous value. In other words be free, for the time being, from the obvious restrictions and limitations of the medium – all those lead lines, metal supports, colour control – and simply paint a picture and feel free to experiment with your ideas. To give you some idea of this I have brought with me another fine book of Marc Chagall's windows, and it does show you to perfection what I mean. Please do look at it later if you want. Also I will show a few slides both of the first paintings and examples of the finished glass, at which stage there may be questions covering points I have failed to make clear. Suffice it to say now that this 'first painting' should not be too glossy an affair, for one is to lead up to the glass being the important finale, which must not in any event become a mere copy of the maquette.

In fact I did find this stage a little difficult since it is at this point that the designs must be submitted for approval and your clients are not necessarily endowed with all that amount of imagination! Even so, with some bright encouragement from yours truly I did get the go ahead and we were in business.

I should like at this stage to say a word or two about this free and easy approach to the preliminary designs, since I believe that the lack of it explains, to a very large extent, the decline in the standard of stained glass all over Europe during the 18th, 19th and first half of the 20th centuries. I am sticking my neck out here, but it would seem that indeed this is the very period when we know that the maquette or cartoon was very precisely and carefully drawn out, painted, shaded in every detail and generally polished to the 'nth' degree, leaving the glazier simply the unenviable job of copying it all on to glass. Well, to begin with one knows just how difficult copying is: the line dies when you are obliged to make it exactly like the original, and also of course glass behaves quite differently from paint on white paper, so that it is small wonder that the glass produced during this long period is so often without spontaneity, life or humour. The faces are all so saintly and perfect, hands without blemish, endless haloes and immaculate gowns – quite unlike the marvellously lively and human little tales told in the great windows of the Middle Ages, really priceless glimpses of the artist himself, tiny animals and gleeful devils – one can find examples everywhere in these earlier periods. And now during this second half of this century life has come back into stained glass again with the work of Chagall, Cecil Collins, Rouault, Fernand Leger, John Piper to name but a few, not to mention the many fabulous abstract painters in glass – men like Alfred Manessier and Patrick Reyntiens himself.

But I had better get back to my own 'free and easy' maquette which I had painted in gouache on paper to a scale of one quarter the final size. For it is now that one does have to do some 'taming' to bring the thing in line with the medium. So to the drawing in of the CUT LINES for the eventual leading. I found it helpful to cover each painting with tracing paper and, following the design beneath, begin drawing the main divisions of colour with charcoal lines. It is important also that these lead-lines make an attractive pattern in themselves, for they should ADD to the character of the window and not just be a necessary evil. Common sense does come into things a good deal here, for we all know the ease with which glass will fracture when being cut, and certain shapes won't work! For instance, one cannot get away with an inward angle – it must be greatly softened. However, the glazier knows a great deal about these problems and quickly notices any impossibilities. Gradually, therefore, the cut lines begin to solve the problem of colour change and allow for the next stage to take place – a COLOUR CHART.

Each proposed colour must now be given a number or letter for identification and the right number written into each piece of the jigsaw, for from this the glazier must calculate the quantity of each colour required. The inevitable wastage while cutting the glass is legion and a good glazier will know his limitations and make appropriate allowances, for once ordered and the glass received, to run out of a colour spells disaster and a terrible hold up of the work.

Now the all-important visit to the GLASS MANUFACTURER – for us quite an outing involving a couple of nights away to allow time to check all those vital and expensive decisions! A most stimulating and awe-inspiring experience for me to see the glass being actually manufactured in so many colours – furnaces and pots of molten glass everywhere. We were able to watch the actual blowing, laying out and cooling of the sheets, to ask questions about the metal oxides used for the different tints, their limitations and strengths – all done by hand with enormous care and precision.

It is at this stage that I must tell you of the two different kinds of antique glass available, POT GLASS and FLASH GLASS. Pot glass is blown from simple single colours, where the colour is spread throughout the substance of the glass and taken from only one pot of molten material. Flash is made from a large amount of base colour, white or lightly tinted, which before it is blown is immediately dipped into a pot of some dark colour at a greater temperature for greater fluidity, and the two layers of glass are blown out together to form a thick base glass with a thick skin of colour on one side. Originally this was done to gain greater transparency with certain colours, particularly for the reds, but this flash glass is also the key to so much wonderment. It allows for some or all of the thin layer of colour to be removed by the application of acid – pure magic, or of course disaster when you burn yourself! This type of glass therefore does also mean an added complication back at the factory, since one must always be thinking: do we need to be able to *attack* that area of the design or can we manage with ordinary pot glass? For, as you may already have guessed, flash glass is considerably more costly than pot glass.

Choice is therefore pretty difficult and the job enormously helped by a good assistant. He is the man who must know all the glass available on the day, the quantities in stock, etc., and be able to quickly bring you samples of the colours, setting up combinations and solutions but without being overpowering. You may imagine he needs to be very clever indeed not to become as confused as the artist; and just when you think you've done it he comes back and says 'not quite enough after all' of the vital link colour. However, eventually the order is made and home you go to await delivery.

While waiting, however, there are the CARTOONS to be made. A cartoon is drawn on to paper measured to the exact size of the finished window, and I mean exact, for it is from this drawing that the actual templates are cut – the templates used by the glazier for each individual piece of glass.

127

Imposing a grid on to the original quarter-sized tracing paper showing the cut lines, one simply copies those cut lines on to the enlarged grid on the cartoon – known by me as 'squaring off', a method for enlarging any design. And one writes the relevant colour number on each space once again. There is now a good deal of setting up to be done in the studio; one needs lots of table space in order to lay out the cartoons and eventually the cut pieces of glass.

Armed with a pair of very special double-bladed scissors, one must cut out each individual piece of the jigsaw. The double blade magically takes out, in the form of a narrow strip of paper, the vital space which must eventually be filled by the lead (approximately 2 millimetres, I guess). As you cut up the cartoon you tack each piece in its position on the table, and as you do that the master glazier can choose all the bits with number 1 2 3 on them and begin cutting from the relevant sheet of glass. And so before your eyes, slowly but surely your very own design begins to take shape in glass, but oh so very far from what you meant, very flat and horribly bright, but nevertheless your own!

There are two methods of allowing you to see what you are doing from now on – one is to stick each piece on to a large glass screen or actual windows with blue tack; or, the other, to arrange a sheet of glass supported by a few books at each end a few inches above your table covered with white paper, and illuminate the gap with strip lights. Now it all looks even worse and work must begin at once to try somehow to impose some discipline and sense of meaning on to these miles of glowing colour.

Stage 1 is to ATTACK the flash glass, and here you need your wits about you – the process is slow and dangerous, and once done cannot be undone and therefore is full of vital decisions. I can go on about this process at length but probably it is enough to say

that the acid used is hydrofluoric, which is extremely dangerous and must be worked on in the open air. Wear plenty of protective clothing and keep well away from children for starters! However, the result of being able to rub away some of the colour on a single piece of glass or indeed actually etch shapes into the glass enormously enlarges your scope. I shall hope to show you some examples when we look at the slides quite soon now.

Stage 2 is the actual PAINTING. Again a very complex business with endless possibilities. I shall try to explain the two most obviously important uses of paint. The compound comes in powder form, which is in fact a mixture of glass oxide and iron oxide mixed to a smooth paste with water and a little gum. The wet mix is then ground for as long as your patience or arm will last, using a Muller and a glass slab. The Muller is rather beautiful, being shaped like a solid glass bell with the broad bottom end being ground exceedingly flat and the top part being the handle. The paint can then be applied in myriad different ways – brushes, fingers, scrumpled paper or plastic, anything to get the effect required. I recall using fingers most. The purpose however is really negative painting: to stop or hold the light, to make passages dim by contrast with those left clear, and so indeed control that riot of brightness so easily brash. The second main use of the paint is to actually draw, i.e. faces, hands, designs, etc., and this is best done as in Chinese calligraphy, holding the brush loosely and attempting a fluid spontaneous effect. It is easy to detect a master at this, for the technique is very difficult and it takes a long time to achieve fluency, I reckon!

The painted piece must then be fired in an oven, or more correctly a kiln with a thermostat, unlike ancient times… It takes the kiln a long time to reach the required temperature of between 450°C and

480°C and then once turned off it must be allowed to cool endlessly, at any rate overnight, before you can open it and check whether all your subtleties have worked, or indeed you must re-cut some pieces and start again. This is when the long-suffering glazier took on his Godly role, since it would be certainly my fault if it hadn't worked, unless of course the kiln over-heated, or something unlikely.

Stage 3 – and you must be wondering if it would ever come – STAINING, the name given to the whole process, but in fact only one quite small part of the work involved. Staining is another mix, this time of silver nitrate and gamboges – the resin taken from a tree growing in Cambodia giving a yellow dye. Now if that isn't an unlikely story – but I looked it up. Applied with a brush to the unpainted side of the glass and passed again through the firing process in the kiln, this unlikely solution, when washed, leaves a most magical golden yellow stain to your window, highlighting certain passages and of course allowing for a third colour on a piece of flash glass. This was the last thing that I, the painter, was allowed to do – and all this, together with all the failures and regrets, eventually leads up to the great and long-suffering guru being left alone to accomplish the marvellous craft of actually setting all the pieces into lead, a craft requiring at least five years of apprenticeship and far longer to be really good, for poor glazing ruins all the effort gone before and in addition will fall to pieces before many hundred years are up!

And then, having sealed all those perfect welds and polished all the fingerprints away, all he must do is to go joyously to the site and erect it all.

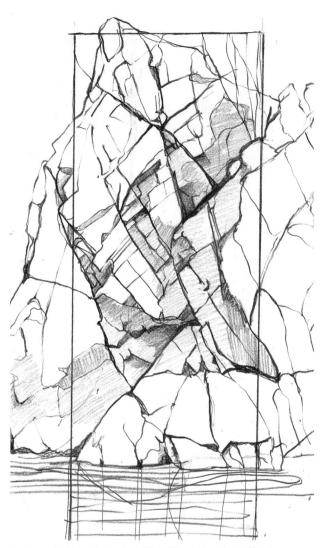

Rock study, Pencil drawing 37 x 33cm, Family Collection

129

Obituary

Reprinted with permission from The Independent, *Obituaries 19 September 2002*

Susan Macfarlane

The death of Susan Macfarlane in an accident outside her studio has robbed the world of a singularly gifted artist. 'She was unique,' says Dr Geoffrey Farrer-Brown, the histopathologist who had worked closely with Macfarlane on exhibitions of her pictures. 'No one else is quite of her calibre in painting medicine at work.'

The recognition that Macfarlane had achieved in a relatively short time in this specialized field became evident early last year when two of her shows were specially requested for the First European Forum on the Arts in Hospitals and Healthcare, Strasbourg. This was launched by the then British Culture Secretary, Chris Smith, and his French counterpart.

The two exhibitions were 'A Picture of Health', on breast-cancer care, originally launched at the Barbican Centre in 1995, and 'Living with Leukaemia', paintings and drawings on childhood leukaemia, given its first showing there in 1998. The meeting of Farrer-Brown and Macfarlane which led to 'A Picture of Health' gave a new twist to her career, already distinguished by its variety and enterprise.

Susan Macfarlane was born in 1938, in Hove, Sussex. She and her brother were brought up on the family farm at Swanmore, Hampshire, and Susan attended Winchester School of Art under David Pare. For several years she had a secretarial job at the Foreign Office, of which she said little, which took her to Sri Lanka and South-East Asia. She continued to paint, holding solo exhibitions at the Times of Ceylon Gallery, in Colombo, and at the Exhibition Hall, Hong Kong. After she moved to Greece, she lived in her friend William Burman's house on the island of Hydra and painted solidly with a local artist, John Dragoumis, an important influence.

In 1964, Susan married Captain Ronald Mackay, much her senior and a friend of her parents. He had had a distinguished naval career and in retirement worked for the marine-engineering firm Foster Wheeler. Susan later told me that she had 'developed very much on my own while living in a remote area of France for 20 years'. She and Ronald initially lived in Cannes, where he had a house, later moving to La Souche, in the Var.

While in Cannes she met the master glazier Alain Peinado, which led her to create 35 square metres of stained glass for the Holy Trinity Church there. Her depiction of the Trinity was only embarked upon after she had, typically, learned exactly how the job would be accomplished from her drawing through to finished window.

Macfarlane had a lifelong love of nature, especially in its most elemental forms, which also prompted her to paint the powerful rock formations and tree shapes of the Alpes-Maritimes.

With the education of their two sons, Euan and Angus, in mind, in 1978 the Mackays moved to Biddestone, Wiltshire, living three months in England, nine in France. Wiltshire fostered Macfarlane's interest in painting pictures related to its ancient cultures and archaeology. An exhibition, 'Ancient Wiltshire', was held at the archaeological museum in Devizes. She was later to have another solo show there, 'An Artist in Ancient Gozo', based on a 1991 visit to Malta and the neolithic temple excavations at Gigantija. A similar subject that attracted her was the prehistoric Pictish stones of Scotland.

In 1986 the Mackays settled in England at Brimscombe, Gloucestershire, where Susan remained until two years ago. The woollen mills of Stroud were nearby, which led Macfarlane to concentrate on people at work. Although it was a relatively new departure for her, this was an honourable theme approached by many artists in different ways. In modern times alone, one can cite Stanley Anderson's long series of meticulously accurate and beautifully composed engravings of country craftsmen of the 1920s and 1930s, the work of war artists such as Stanley Spencer in the shipyards of Port Glasgow or the sculptor Ghisha Koenig's more recent bronzes and terracottas of tentmakers and glassworkers. Macfarlane's 'The Woollen Mills of Stroud', held in the town's Subscription Rooms in 1991, was featured on the BBC Radio 4 programme *Woman's Hour*.

A meeting with Geoffrey Farrer-Brown in 1992 led him to propose that Macfarlane should record on site the sensitive and sometimes little-understood clinical treatment of breast cancer. The resulting Barbican Centre exhibition attracted much attention, the paintings of unique sensitivity being featured on the BBC2 television programme *Newsnight*, fully vindicating Farrer-Brown's inspiration. Again,

Macfarlane was following in a worthy tradition that included such artists as Henry Tonks and Barbara Hepworth.

When the Royal Mail was drawing up plans for Millennium stamps, it chose a Macfarlane breast-cancer image for the 26p issue. 'Because none of the paintings for the exhibition fitted the stamp, they got her to specially paint a post-operative recovery picture for the series', says Farrer-Brown.

Like 'Living with Leukaemia', 'A Picture of Health' has continued to tour since its inception. It will next be seen at the Guildhall, Winchester, from 27 September until 12 October, and goes to a hospital in Waterford, Ireland, next spring. Farrer-Brown foresees more venues after that.

The 1990s saw Macfarlane's 'delight in atmosphere and mystery' drawing her back to landscape, and there was a series exploring ideas from the sea. She returned to her people-at-work theme in 1996 with pictures completed at the malt whisky distillery Balblair, where the copper vats fascinated her. The distillery owners bought the pictures, which are on display.

Macfarlane was at the height of her powers when she died and had already started on a third medical exhibition for Farrer-Brown called 'Blindness and sight'. 'She had done the first five paintings, the last four in conjunction with consultants at Moorfields Hospital' – perhaps a quarter of the projected show.

David Buckman

Susan Macfarlane, artist: born Hove, Sussex 17 June 1938; married 1964 Ronald Mackay (died 1991; two sons); died Petersfield, Hampshire 14 August 2002.

Acknowledgements

Special thanks to Alan Caiger-Smith for agreeing
to review Susan's work and for the way in which
he has managed to convey so many of her qualities
as a painter.

Thanks to Jane Knott for kindly editing the text.

We would also like to thank the following people for
their contribution to the production of this book:

Angela Angel
William Burman
Geoffrey Farrer-Brown
Michael Macfarlane
Anna Mackay
Alain Peinado
Susie Walker

Also to all those who lent their paintings to be
photographed: Angela Angel, Diana Arfaras,
Balblair Distillery, Eileen Burbidge, William Burman,
Deidre Clenet, Brian de Soissons, Charlotte
Earnshaw, Sue and George Edwards, Geoffrey Farrer-
Brown, Mavora Forward, Jerry Gilmore, Derek and
Sonia Hornby, Inverhouse Distillery, Joan Osmond,
Alain and Monique Peinado, Michael Ross, Anne
Shepherd, Stephen and Susannah Skurray, Sarah
Thomas, and James and Fiona Wickham.

Thanks to the Royal Mail for the reproduction
of the *Nursing Care* Millennium stamp on page 17.

132

Book published by Euan and Angus Mackay

Cover image: *Dance of Life (A Celebration of Life)*

Photography: Black Sheep Media, Clarissa Bruce, Geoffrey Farrer-Brown, Brian Hallam,
    Barry Lewis, Richard Littlewood, Brenton McGeachie, Jean-Claude Ratignier,
    Chris Rose and Stephen Skurray

Design: Eyelevel Design Consultants

Print: BAS Printers, Salisbury

ISBN 0-9550438-0-8